Thoughts
from the
Heart

Annie Barlow Deberry

Thoughts
from the
Heart

by

Annie Barlow Deberry

LOWBAR
PUBLISHING COMPANY

905 South Douglas Avenue • Nashville, Tennessee 37204
Phone: 615-972-2842
E-mail: Lowbarpublishingcompany@gmail.com
Web site: www.Lowbarbookstore.com

Lowbar Publishing Company

Nashville, Tennessee 37204

615-972-2842

E-mail:Lowbarpublishingcompany@gmail.com

Website: www.Lowbarbookstore.com

For additional information, workshop, and seminars contact the author as following:

Annie Barlow Deberry

Phone: 252-908-3337

E-mail: abd4000@aol.com

Author: Annie Barlow Deberry

Copy Editor: Olivia Cloud

Photos: Calvin C. Barlow, Jr. and Microsoft Clip Art

Graphic and Cover Design Artist: Norah S. Branch

Table of Contents

Dedication vi

The Pen 2

You Thought 4

Conversations of the Mind 6

Darkness in the Daylight 8

Guilty from my Viewpoint 10

It's About Time 12

Master 14

Maturity 16

Moving Personalities 18

Wrapped in Faith 20

Permission Granted or Taken for Granted 22

Praying in Advance for Insurance Needed 24

The Pain of It All 26

Sometimes 28

A Never-Ending Ride 30

Thoughts from the Heart 32

About the Authoer 34

Dedication

Thoughts from the Heart is dedicated to the memory of my wonderful parents, my loving and devoted husband, our lovely children and my supportive siblings. It is this circle of love and God's grace and mercy that allows me to humbly grow and blossom within and share with others.

How to Use As an Educational Tool

The author's overall vision for the optimum utilization of *Thoughts from the Heart* involves the reader adding his or her artistic or poetic insight into the poems. The concept is to have the reader visualize each poem's meaning as it applies to a relevant time in his or her life or environment. This will allow the reader to captivate and expound upon personal talents. This approach is both affirming and inviting, as it does not assume a right or wrong answer; but rather, simply invites an answer or thought.

This exercise would be ideal for a classroom setting because it can be a catalyst to inspire students to write a story or paragraph based upon a personal interpretation of the poem. This approach has the potential to strengthen the students' comprehension, grammar, and creative and critical thinking skills.

The students' artistic skills also could be enhanced by illustrating their perspective of the poems on canvas.

These poems also can provide personal insight and inspiration as you answer and generate your own questions after reading the poems. For example:

1. Am I using my natural talents?
2. What inspires my viewpoints on life?
3. Do I sometimes listen with my heart?
4. How do I take control of my destiny?
5. What life processes are building my foundation?
6. Do I allow society to compromise my fundamental beliefs?
7. Do I solicit help?

In summary, readers will have the opportunity to go on an interactive journey and draw a picture or write statements. You also may choose to sit back, relax and just enjoy the rhythm of the poetic lines. *Thoughts from the Heart* is sure to inspire the poetic and artistic capabilities that dwell within you.

The Pen

Gifts from above are expressed in natural forms.

Never let loyalty and faithfulness leave you.
Tie them around your neck;
write them on the tablet of your heart.
(Proverbs 3:3, HCSB)

The Pen

The pen inks what it sees and feels.

It ignores the rules of the basic five senses.

It is fueled by pain, compassion, joy and sadness within.

The pen embraces its rhythm and moves to a different calling.

I surrender, helpless to its topics and jargons;

Eagerly awaiting the announcement
of the next journey or adventure.

It is certain to reveal pain, compassion, joy or sadness;

Perhaps a cry of thunder overruled by a signature
of happiness or a bid farewell.

Life erupts and a new evolvement is on the horizon;

I dare not take a bow, boast or put on a tiara.

The gift of the pen in this season;
credits are rained down from above.

All gratitude, praise and accolades belong to Him.

Annie Barlow Deberry 7/8/14

You Thought

In spite of others thoughts, we are accountable for personal choices.

How magnificent are Your works, Lord, how profound Your thoughts!

(Psalm 92:5, HCSB)

You Thought

You thought I answered a question in the affirmative,
based upon your being;

This mind sails a sea not charted by
your longitudes, latitudes and windstorms.

You thought it was imperative that I read from your pages
and follow that pathway;

Take another look at the equipment and ability
given to one who seeks the truth.

You thought your way was laid out with clarity
and could not be defaulted;.

My course of action demands a thinker
of realism built on a firm foundation.

You thought what was said, done and documented
must be my only direction;

The real Teacher's book is the knowledge
that appeals to my heart and soul.

You thought that temporary promises
would bind me to the chains of life;

I am destined to greater with a mindset
that views the earthly end as the beginning.

Annie Barlow Deberry 6/10/14

Conversations of the Mind

**Sometimes the best conversations
are communicated in silence.**

*For who has known the Lord's mind,
that he may instruct Him?
But we have the mind of Christ.*

(1 Corinthians 2:16, NKJV)

Conversations of the Mind

Words formed into thoughts never to be uttered out loud,

A silent conversation every time we have an encounter,

An interpreter or sign language is not required for this episode.

Your curtain is pulled down
and somehow you secured the door locks.

It seems like a mental waste to engage in this activity,

Yet it must be played out with each word and gesture.

This action and reaction is repeated often throughout our duration;

It finds me once again drained, weak
and releasing the river from my eyes in secret.

My weapon of choice remains the same and equips me daily,

It prepares me for the battle and gives me hope;

Tomorrow we will speak and rejoice before our top becomes snow,

Perhaps our final dialogue is destined to happen in the clouds.

Annie Barlow Deberry 7/3/14

Darkness in the Daylight

Sometimes darkness shines in daylight's moments.

And the light shines in the darkness,
and the darkness did not comprehend it.
(John 1:5, NKJV)

Darkness in the Daylight

The sun's rays are smiling so radiantly that the warmth heats my bones;
My heart struggles to see the daylight
because every valve is blocked with mental anguish and agony.

Sunglasses are required to exit the building to prevent glare damage;
The depth of my soul shouts for vision in the bright spotlight.

I hurt so deeply within that the doctor continues
to misdiagnose the symptoms;
The blindness is not hereditary, nor genetically charged from the womb.

The light and sea provided a gateway of love
within and your arrival illuminated our world;

I put aside my welder's goggles to embrace the glow
to find a pathway in the morning hours.

The wound radiates through the darkness
with a force unmatched by the strongest waterfall;

I seek shelter in the caves of life
to ponder my next move and preparation.

A flood of light rushes in at the doorway of the tunnel,
This signifies that I was not alone on this journey
even though the footsteps were silent.

My voice echoed through the darkness in the daylight
and the war within ceases to exist.

Annie Barlow Deberry 7/6/14

Guilty from My Viewpoint

If loving, nurturing, and caring are sins, then I am guilty.

Train up a child in the way he should go,
And when he is old he will not depart from it.
(Proverbs 22:6, NKJV)

Guilty from My Viewpoint

Guilty as charged of being a caring and loving parent.

Guilty as charged of wanting to see you excel in life.

Guilty as charged of introducing you to a better way of life.

Guilty as charged of sharing the values of strong work ethics.

Guilty as charged of teaching you about self-respect
and respect for others.

Guilty as charged of bringing you up in a Sunday school environment.

Guilty as charged of sharing the joy
of knowing Jesus Christ for yourself.

Guilty as charged of feeling your pain and sadness.

Guilty as charged of rejoicing in your successes and happiness.

Guilty as charged of trying to protect you from falling and failures.

Guilty as charged of having a difficult time letting you go,
grow and make unnecessary mistakes.

Guilty as charged of sometimes viewing you
as my toddler instead of a young adult.

Guilty as charged of praying for you daily
and often throughout the day.

I choose to remain guilty from my viewpoint.

Annie Barlow Deberry 6/29/14

It's About Time

Time is a valuable resource.

To everything there *is a season,*
A time for every purpose under heaven:
(Ecclesiastes 3:1, NKJV)

It's About Time

It's about time I awake and see the beauty.

It's about time I acknowledge the given inner strength.

It's about time I put behind the hidden weight.

It's about time I choose to move forward toward the daylight.

It's about time I fully embrace the responsibilities
of my chronological date.

It's about time I take the path filled with unchartered choices
and boldly open the gate.

It's about time I take a stand and enlarge the universe with hope,
health, wealth and happiness.

It's about time!!!

Annie Barlow Deberry 7/8/14

Master

Sometimes needs determine our master.

No one can serve two masters; for either he will hate the one and love the other, or else he will be loyal to the one and despise the other. You cannot serve God and mammon.
(Matthew 6:24, NKJV)

Master

I once thought at a tender age, before wisdom's years,
that the mirror's reflection was the master;

The curtain of life peeled backed layers uncovering
and unveiling renditions to songs never played.

Master, it has to be the mirror's reflection not understanding
the consequences of every song;

One now wants to seek shelter and hide under the cover
of protection until the music of life stops.

Master, life **won't** let me consciously pick the selections and folly
without the realization of a fall;

I own my awakened stage and the responsibility
that engulfs the environment so delicately designated.

Master, the path was documented and the map read
with a blinded focus to create a false win;

The time will come when the lyrics will be played back
to the mirror's reflection.

Master, the time of acknowledgment will wipe away
the ill-fitted shoes and allow the dance to begin;

This is the importance of musical selections in a timely manner
to yield the desired calculated results.

Annie Barlow Deberry 6/29/14

Maturity

Maturity is not measured by longevity.

I, therefore, the prisoner of the Lord,
beseech you to walk worthy of the calling with
which you were called, with all lowliness and gentleness,
with longsuffering, bearing with one another in love,
endeavoring to keep the unity of the Spirit
in the bond of peace.

(Ephesians 4:1-3, NKJV)

Maturity

Maturity is not based upon age; but rather upon actions.

Maturity is not measured by how fast you run from the situation;
but rather, by how quickly you face it.

Maturity is not built upon lies and guilt;
but rather, upon ownership and acceptance.

Maturity is not denial, but rather, acknowledgement.

Maturity invites an open environment for discussion,
not negative, close-minded debates.

Maturity begins in the mind and ends with the physical steps
to solidify cohesion.

Maturity is not always right or wrong or even black or white.

Maturity does not happen overnight; but rather,
develops over time with dedicated nurturing.

Maturity lies within your control of selections.

Annie Barlow Deberry 7/2/14

Moving Personalities

Sometimes people are like the waves of the ocean.

For God is not the author of confusion but of peace,

(1 Corinthians 14:33, NKJV)

Moving Personalities

This morning was sunny and your smile was beaming brightly;
The blinds surely must be fully opened or missing.
Your body language pronounced and enunciated every syllable;
Seconds later a cloud of mixed emotions
moves in and the set changes.
It is not surprising that the main characters
step back in observation;
Time and time again this is played out without a producer's script;
A mere toddler's tantrum with an upscale age accountability twist.
Awareness and responsibility are selectively missing by choice;
Actions direct a reaction of sadness and confusion,
The mental waiting game begins with the onset of your next move.
Hesitation filled with anticipation as the scene unfolds,
The main characters remain oblivious
because of a forecasted emotional storm.
It is clear that you know where to seek shelter within the zone,
Choose and take control today to end, and not extend,
the moving personalities within.

Annie Barlow Deberry 6/29/14

Wrapped in Faith

Faith is always shining.

For we walk by faith, not by sight.

(2 Corinthians 5:7, NKJV)

Wrapped in Faith

In the growing years, it was clear that you marched
to the beat of a different drummer;

While maturity in excess of every birthday
was displayed so eloquently.

No bells or whistles alerted the parental authority
of a higher calling;

Reflections on past years are now indicative
that the preparation was underway.

Each room in your abode decorated with His word
as a reminder of your devotion;

Your approach to life's challenges is resounding
because it emulated your beliefs.

This was transparent and displayed through
your announcement as a cancer survivor.

A true first born, a leader in your own right guided by His light,

Strengthened daily to release and share it
with others through powerful prayers.

A inspiration of hope, comfort and a designated prayer warrior,

A true deliverer of His word and acceptance of the tasks.

Picket signs never required as you advocate love
and justice in your heart for all;

A beautiful sweet spirited young woman draped
with such unwavering faith.

Annie Barlow Deberry 7/17/14

Permission Granted or Taken for Granted

Gratitude is beauty expressed with words.

Enter into His gates with thanksgiving, And *into His courts with praise. Be thankful to Him,* and *bless His name.*

(Psalm 100:4, NKJV)

Permission Granted or Taken for Granted

It is no mystery why many are confused with the phrases
"permission granted" and "taken for granted."
Living in a society with such daily hustling and a me-and-mine mentality,
I willingly received you into my world, permission granted
or taken for granted.
Changed, cleaned and prayed for you,
permission granted or taken for granted.
Prepared your food and read you bedtime stories,
permission granted or taken for granted.
Protected and stood up for your voice to be heard,
permission granted or taken for granted.
The clock ticks and you exceed a decade plus
and comprehend well beyond your years.
Sacrifices are made without a simple thank you,
permission granted or taken for granted.
Your requests are met and dreams intact,
permission granted or taken for granted.
Unwilling at times to share a conversation or embrace,
permission granted or taken for granted.
Funds are dispersed on your behalf at the expense of others,
permission granted or taken for granted.
Beliefs reveal that behaviors determine the outcome of
permission granted or taken for granted.

Annie Barlow Deberry   7/6/2014

Praying in Advance for Insurance Needed

Insurance is a prayer in advance of a need.

Watch and pray, lest you enter into temptation.
The spirit indeed is willing, but the flesh is weak.

(Matthew 26:41, NKJV)

Praying in Advance for Insurance Needed

Pain is a simple four-letter word that is very powerful and
controlling;
Pain's mental foothold has far-reaching arms that extend beyond
the range of many;
Pain has the potential to dangle your past like a never-ending
pendulum;
Pain cripples your mind and desires to render you hopeless and
wandering;
Pain does not take exception to age, race, creed or color;
Pain articulates in a manner of great and absolute authority;
Pain will cause you to cry out in the midst of a sound sleep;
Pain silences your smile, inner song and youthful expression;
Pain surrenders and takes a back seat to a faith-based prayer;
Pain's power ceases and releases the grip and acknowledges the
call of One.
Pain's zeal diminishes when **P**raying in **A**dvance for **I**nsurance
Needed.

Annie Barlow Deberry 7/6/2014

The Pain of It All

Seeing them grow is worth the pain.

Behold, children are a heritage from the Lord.

(Psalm 127:3, NKJV)

The Pain of it All

I graciously welcomed and cherished the nine-month figure.

The tears, delight, anguish and sleepless nights,

Years of laughing, crying and watching you flourish on
and off the sideline,

Your number one fan, cheerleader, negotiator,
and prayer intercessor.

All this was done with great finesse and love,

Now the tables turn and your voice is sounding,

Your direction is not driven by my heartbeat and inner vision;

Outside noises quicken and arouse your curiosity
with a strong magnet;

Your steps are sometimes influenced by others,
without your eternal view in sight.

My continuing cycle remains constant,
with a greater emphasis as a prayer intercessor;

The fork of life happens and the reality is the joy
that binds the pain of it all.

Annie Barlow Deberry 6/24/2014

Sometimes

Everything and everybody need sometimes.

*You will show me the path of life; In Your presence is fullness of
joy; At Your right hand are pleasures forevermore.*

(Psalm 16:11, NKJV)

Sometimes

Sometimes the morning sun brings an array of choices
filled with endless solutions;

On those days my mind speeds to the front of the line,
only to wait for the rushes of life to pass by.

Sometimes I awake from the soundness of sleep
to hear the answers to questions never asked;

This mind of mine is allowed to go places
without limits and restrictions.

Sometimes a passing conversation sparks a flood of thoughts;

The directions and influences of life carry you
to the light and darkness.

Sometimes a harness is put on to bring us back to
the atmosphere of existence;

Then the recognition is made clear that
the inhale-and-exhale process waits for no one.

Sometimes I wonder if ocean waves will wash
to the seashore obstacles or opportunities;

Now the truth reveals the known to the unknown
while staging the answer in the confirmatory.

Annie Barlow Deberry 6/8/14

A Never-Ending Ride

Marriage is an extension of a courtship with bliss.

He who finds a wife finds a good thing,
and obtains favor from the Lord.

(Proverbs 18:22, NKJV)

A Never-Ending Ride

It appeared to unobserving eyes to be a simple ride
on a Ferris wheel between two;

Though the undercurrent to unfold would become the ignition
of a beautiful blessing,

An unassuming but gentle introduction combined with a smile
and touch of hands.

Now the two unknowingly were on their journey
to becoming one in the not-so-distance future,

A youthful harmony in the ending year of high school
set the stage of glow and delight;

That blissful prom night where the dancing, music
and the moon all belong to your endless memories.

The pursuit of a higher education and career created
a brief interruption of the physical bonding;

This allowed time for the heart and mind
to grow a strong and lovely affection.

The enchanting telephone calls and mountain
of marvelous love letters became the foundation;

Seemingly the years passed quickly and the reuniting occurred
with a deeper commitment.

Like a whirlwind, the asking of hands, engagement
and heavenly wedding remain a divine reality;

The two continue to thrive as one blessed by God above
and added four to the circle of love.

Annie Barlow Deberry 7/10/14

Thoughts from the Heart

Thoughts from the Heart is a collection of poems comprised of experiences, revelations and observations. The poems are written to engage and inspire the reader as he or she reflects on its application to their specific circumstances or environment. This interactive journey centers on having the ability to draw a picture or write statements. You may also choose to sit back, relax and just enjoy the rhythmic poetic offerings. *Thoughts from the Heart* is sure to bring out the poetic and artistic capabilities that dwell within every reader.

About the Author

Annie Virginia Barlow Deberry is a native of Ripley, Tennessee. She is the daughter of the late Calvin Coolidge Barlow, Sr. and Annie Cathryn Johnson Barlow, the middle child among fifteen siblings. She is married to Robert Deberry, Sr., also from Tennessee. They are the proud parents of RoVirginette, Robert, Jr., Johnson and Cathryn Deberry. Robert and Annie currently reside in Rocky Mount, North Carolina, where they are active members of Ebenezer Missionary Baptist Church. Annie is also a member of Zeta Phi Beta Sorority, Incorporated.

At an early age, Annie enjoyed reading and writing poetry. Writing seemingly always allowed her an avenue to express her emotions and visions. She found writing assignments throughout her educational and career endeavors gratifying, though challenging at times.

Annie graduated from Ripley High School. After graduation, she earned a Bachelor of Science degree in Chemistry from LeMoyne-Owen College, located in Memphis. Annie obtained her Master of Business Administration in Applied Management from Indiana Wesleyan University, situated in Marion, Indiana. She is currently pursuing a Doctor of Christian Counseling degree from Andersonville Theological Seminary.

Annie's work career started when she was sixteen as a gift wrapper with Guttmann's department store. She worked with S&R of Tennessee during her high school senior year as a factory worker.

Annie's college co-op began with International Harvester as a laboratory technician during her undergraduate years, and with Jackson State University as a research intern using mass spectrometry. She was employed as a production engineer with GTE Sylvania in Dyersburg, Tennessee. She worked for Cummins Rocky Mount Engine Plant in leadership roles as a chemistry lab engineer, and as a team, business, and quality manger. Annie retired in 2012 after thirty-one years of service and accomplishments.

CPSIA information can be obtained at www.ICGtesting.com
Printed in the USA
BVOW11s1447060115

382115BV00002B/2/P